THIS BOOK BELONGS TO

_____

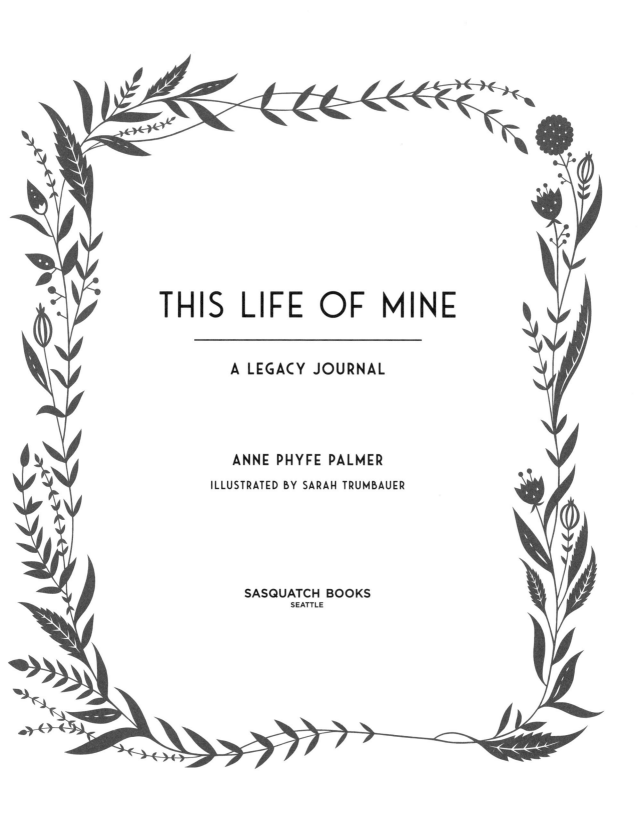

THIS LIFE OF MINE

A LEGACY JOURNAL

ANNE PHYFE PALMER

ILLUSTRATED BY SARAH TRUMBAUER

SASQUATCH BOOKS
SEATTLE

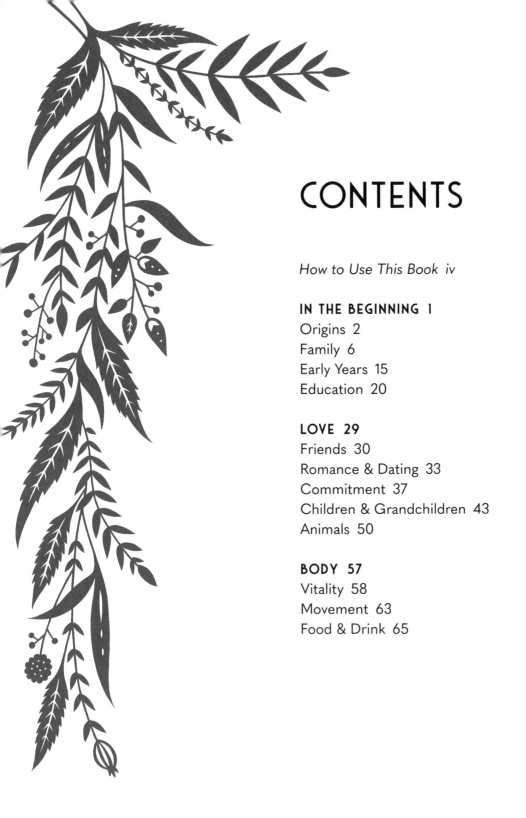

CONTENTS

HOW TO USE THIS BOOK

Welcome to *This Life of Mine*. This book was designed for personal enjoyment but also to leave behind a legacy of words and stories and images. You can come and go, dropping in where you wish—just keep coming back to preserve those special memories. Your stories are waiting to be remembered and revisited. In the retelling, they will offer you and your loved ones insights into the life you've lived and the paths you've traveled.

To that end, have fun—write and doodle and approach each section in whatever way feels right—but aim to finish. Here are some tips for how to get the most out of your time with this book:

1. Consider reading this book from start to finish before you begin to write.

2. Write somewhere you enjoy: a well-lit space in your home, a favorite coffee shop, a library reading room.

3. Write when you have food in your belly: Writing takes brain energy, especially writing that involves making choices. Refuel as needed!

4. Clear your head before you write. Take a few deep breaths, or meditate if it's a practice you are familiar with.

5. Get started with a section that appeals to you to get your pen flowing (and use a pen you enjoy).

6. First thought equals best thought. The prompts are intended to bring forth responses and memories that may be hidden in your subconscious. Try not to overthink your answers or aim for perfection.

7. Skip prompts and return to them later if they are holding you up. Want to write more? Continue any of your answers at the end of each section in More to Know.

8. Allow yourself to take several passes at each section. You might find it helpful to jump around and answer just a few prompts from each one in a sitting, then return another day to tackle a few more. Not every prompt will be suited to your life; you don't have to answer all of the prompts or fill all of the space!

9. Reward yourself when you've completed a section in full: Go for a walk! Have a cup of tea or a cookie! Call or visit a good friend!

10. Give the book to someone you love, or hold on to it, revisiting and adding to your answers over the years to come.

IN THE BEGINNING

ORIGINS

My given name: ....

The story behind my name: ....
....
....
....

My name now: ....

Where I was born: ....
....

The day and time I was born: ....
....

A story about my birth: ....

....

....

....

....

....

....

....

....

....

My parents' names and birth dates: ....

....

....

Where my parents were born: ....

....

....

....

....

My siblings' names and birth dates: ....

....

....

....

....

My place in the birth order: ....

My grandparents' names, birth dates, and where they were born: ....

....

....

....

....

....

....

....

....

....

My family tree:

FAMILY

Information about my parents and their lives: ....
....
....
....
....
....
....
....
....
....
....
....
....
....
....
....
....

A quirky detail about each of my parents: ....

....

....

....

....

....

....

....

Some facts about my grandparents and their lives: ....

....

....

....

....

....

....

....

....

....

....

....

....

....

A quirky detail about each of my grandparents: ....

....

....

....

....

....

....

....

....

....

....

....

....

....

Other family members who have impacted my life: ....

....

....

....

....

....

....

....

....

....

....

....

....

....

....

Events in history that shaped my family: ....

....

....

....

....

....

....

....

....

....

A significant event in my family's personal history: ....

....

....

....

....

....

....

....

....

....

....

The greatest hardship my family endured: ....
....
....
....
....
....
....

Rituals or traditions my family observed: ....
....
....
....
....
....
....
....
....
....
....

Inspirational stories my family passed down: ....

....

....

....

....

....

....

....

....

....

....

....

....

....

....

....

....

....

Games my family played together: ....

....

....

....

Activities my family participated in together: ....

....

....

....

....

Early dreams that my family discouraged: ....

....

....

....

....

Early dreams that my family supported: ....

....

....

....

....

Something I did as a teenager that my parents never found out about: ....

....

....

....

....

....

The ways I differ from my family: ....

....

....

....

....

....

....

The best things about my family: ....

....

....

....

....

....

....

EARLY YEARS

When I was ____ I looked like this:

A favorite room from my childhood: ....

....

....

....

....

....

....

My beloved stuffed animal, blanket, or other cherished item: ....

....

....

....

....

Things I enjoyed doing after school and on the weekends: ....

....

....

....

....

....

....

....

What summers were like growing up: ....

....

....

....

....

....

....

....

A typical childhood vacation: ....

....

....

....

....

....

....

....

....

....

....

A childhood memory that stands out: ....

....

....

....

....

....

....

....

Where I went to daydream, get away, or be alone: ....

....

....

....

....

....

....

....

My dreams and aspirations when I was a child: ....

....

....

....

....

....

....

....

....

My greatest strength growing up: ....

....

....

....

....

....

A brief summary of my childhood: ....

....

....

....

....

....

EDUCATION

Schools I attended during childhood: ....
....
....
....
....

Teachers I remember most: ....
....
....
....

A teacher who had a great impact on me and why: ....
....
....
....
....
....
....
....
....

My favorite subject(s): ....
....
....

My least favorite subject(s): ....
....
....

Accolades or special experiences: ....
....
....

A memory from school: ....
....
....
....
....
....
....
....

An awkward school moment: ....
....
....
....
....

Activities I enjoyed: ....
....
....
....
....
....

Clubs or groups I belonged to: ....
....
....
....
....
....

Post–high school education, training, or degrees: ....

....

....

....

....

....

....

....

Studies or experiences abroad: ....

....

....

....

....

....

....

....

MORE TO KNOW

....
....
....
....
....
....
....
....
....
....
....
....
....
....

27

FRIENDS

The importance of friendship in my life: ....
....
....
....
....
....

My friends would describe me as: ....
....
....

The friends I have known the longest and how we met: ....
....
....
....
....
....
....
....
....
....

My closest friends as a child: ....
....
....
....
....
....
....

My closest friends as an adult: ....
....
....
....
....
....
....

Friends who have been there for me when I needed them most: ....
....
....
....
....
....
....

How my friends show support: ....
....
....
....
....

The friendships that defy time and distance: ....
....
....
....
....
....

A friend I miss who is no longer in my life: ....
....
....
....
....
....

ROMANCE & DATING

A memory of a childhood crush: ....

....

....

....

....

....

....

....

....

....

A memory of my first date: ....

....

....

....

....

....

....

....

....

....

What dating was like for me: ....
....
....
....
....
....
....
....
....
....
....
....

My time as a single person has been: ....
....
....
....
....
....
....
....
....
....
....
....

An early love interest and what the person and our relationship were like: ....

....

....

....

....

....

....

....

....

....

....

....

....

....

An experience of heartbreak: ....
....
....
....
....
....
....

When I first lived with a lover or partner: ....
....
....

The best part of living with a lover or partner was (or is): ....
....
....
....
....

The hardest part of living with a lover or partner was (or is): ....
....
....
....
....

COMMITMENT

My spouse or partner's name: ....

When and where my spouse or partner was born: ....
....

How and when we met: ....
....
....
....
....
....
....
....
....
....
....
....
....

What drew me to my spouse or partner: ....
....
....
....
....
....
....
....

How our relationship began: ....
....
....
....
....
....
....
....

Where we first lived together: ....
....
....

What we do for fun: ....
....
....
....
....
....

Values we share: ....
....
....
....
....

What I love about my spouse or partner: ....
....
....
....
....
....
....

Our engagement story: ....
....
....
....
....
....
....

Our wedding date and the special details: ....
....
....
....
....,
....
....

Our honeymoon story: ....
....
....
....
....
....

What I love about being married: ....
....
....
....
....
....
....
....
....

What I find challenging about being married: ....
....
....
....
....
....
....
....
....

How we keep our relationship alive or why we couldn't: ....

....

....

....

....

....

....

....

....

Other committed relationships that have been important in my life: ....

....

....

....

....

....

....

....

CHILDREN & GRANDCHILDREN

Names of my own children or special children in my life: ....
....
....
....

When and where they were born: ....
....
....
....
....

What I remember most about first meeting each child: ....
....
....
....
....
....
....
....
....
....

A detail or story about each child: ....
....
....
....
....
....
....
....
....
....
....
....

One or two surprising quotes or actions from their childhoods: ....
....
....
....
....
....
....
....

My relationship with my children: ....

....

....

....

....

....

....

How I have tried to influence my children: ....

....

....

....

....

....

....

How my children have influenced me: ....

....

....

....

....

....

What brings me joy as a parent: ....
....
....
....
....
....
....
....

What has challenged me most as a parent: ....
....
....
....
....
....
....
....

How being a parent changed me: ....

....

....

....

....

....

....

....

....

....

Names of my grandchildren: ....

....

....

....

....

....

....

A detail about each grandchild: ....
....
....
....
....
....
....
....
....
....
....
....
....
....

How being a grandparent changed me: ....
....
....
....
....
....
....

My relationship with my grandchildren: ....
....
....
....
....
....
....

What brings me joy as a grandparent: ....
....
....
....
....
....
....

Other children in my life who are special to me: ....
....
....
....
....
....

ANIMALS

My favorite animals and what I love about them: ....
....
....
....

My favorite pet(s) and why: ....
....
....
....

Other pets and animals that have been a part of my life: ....
....
....
....

What animals bring to my life: ....

....

....

....

....

....

Quirks of some of my pets: ....

....

....

....

....

....

A drawing, photo, or description of the animal I most relate to:

MORE TO KNOW

....
....
....
....
....
....
....
....
....
....
....
....
....
....
....
....
....
....

BODY

VITALITY

What I look like now:

My general health is: ....
....
....

How I start my day: ....
....
....
....
....
....
....
....

My daily rituals: ....
....
....
....
....
....
....
....

Things that make me feel energized and strong: ....

....

....

....

....

....

....

Habits I want to cultivate or give up: ....

....

....

....

....

....

....

Things that help me to be healthy: ....

....

....

....

....

....

....

My minor illnesses or injuries: ....
....
....
....
....

My major illnesses or injuries: ....
....
....
....
....

What helps me manage illness or injury: ....
....
....
....
....
....

Parts of my body I appreciate: ....

....

....

....

A quirky detail about my body: ....

....

....

....

How I feel about aging: ....

....

....

....

....

....

....

....

....

....

....

....

MOVEMENT

Favorite ways and places to move my body: ....
....
....
....
....
....
....
....

What makes me feel most calm and centered: ....
....
....
....
....
....
....

Modes of exercise/movement I have tried: ....

....

....

....

....

Sports I played as a child: ....

....

....

....

What I learned from childhood sports: ....

....

....

....

....

Sports I have played as an adult and why: ....

....

....

....

....

Sports I enjoy watching and why: ....

....

....

....

....

....

Teams or athletes I root for: ....

....

....

....

FOOD & DRINK

Three of my favorite foods as a child: ....

....

....

Memorable meals my parents made when I was a child: ....

....

....

....

Foods I refused to eat as a child: ....

....

My three favorite foods or meals now: ....

....

....

....

Foods I don't eat: ....

....

My favorite comfort food: ....

My favorite snack food: ....

Foods or drinks I associate with specific times in my life: ....

....

....

....

....

Ways my palate has changed over time: ....

....

....

The meals I most like to cook: ....

....

....

....

....

An indispensable cookbook: ....

My favorite beverage: ....

A cuisine or dish I wish I knew how to cook: ....

My menu for a perfect meal and who I would invite: ....

....

....

....

....

....

....

....

....

MORE TO KNOW

....
....
....
....
....
....
....
....
....
....
....
....
....
....
....
....

CREATIVITY & HOBBIES

Ways I express my creativity: ....
....
....
....
....
....
....

My creative process: ....
....
....
....
....
....
....

Teachers, writers, artists, or musicians who have influenced me: ....
....
....
....
....

My hobbies and passions: ....
....
....
....
....
....
....
....
....

If I could be any artist, writer, or musician, I would be: ....
....
....

If I could learn any new hobby, process, or art form, it would be: ....
....
....
....
....
....
....

PERSONAL STYLE

Clothing I remember from my childhood: ....
....
....
....
....

Clothing I wore in my teen years: ....
....
....
....
....

Clothing I have loved in my adult life: ....
....
....
....
....

Colors I like to wear: ....
....
....

My personal style could be described as: ....
....
....

Ways my style has changed over time: ....
....
....
....

Favorite outfits or pieces I wear now: ....
....
....
....

What I wear when I want to feel comfortable: ....
....
....

ART

Favorite art forms: ....
....
....
....
....

Favorite works of art: ....
....
....
....
....

My favorite artists and what I like about their work: ....
....
....
....
....
....
....
....
....

Art I have in my home: ....

....

....

....

....

....

An art piece that is special to me: ....

....

....

....

....

Favorite museums: ....

....

....

....

....

....

My favorite colors: ....

....

BOOKS

The importance of reading in my life: ....
....
....
....
....
....
....
....
....

Books I remember from my childhood: ....
....
....
....
....
....
....
....
....
....
....

My all-time favorite books: ....

....

....

....

....

....

....

....

....

....

Genres I most enjoy: ....

....

....

....

....

My favorite authors: ....

....

....

....

....

....

A fictional character I identify with: ....
....
....
....
....
....
....
....

MUSIC

Instruments I have played: ....
....
....

Instruments I wish I had learned to play: ....
....
....

The first concert I attended: ....

....

....

....

The most memorable concert I attended and why: ....

....

....

....

....

....

....

....

Songs, albums, or bands that were part of my youth: ....

....

....

....

....

....

....

....

Songs, albums, or bands that have been part of my adult life: ....

....

....

....

....

....

....

....

Songs or albums that have been the soundtracks of my life: ....

....

....

....

....

....

....

....

Musicians I've listened to through the years: ....

....

....

....

....

....

....

Musical genres I enjoy: ....

....

....

....

....

Ways my musical taste has changed over time: ....

....

....

....

....

....

....

FILM & TV

Films or TV series I remember from my childhood: ....

....

....

....

....

....

....

....

Films or TV series that have influenced me: ....

....

....

....

....

....

....

....

....

....

....

Films or TV series I believe everyone should see: ....

....

....

....

....

....

....

....

....

....

Favorite movie snack: ....

My film or TV character alter ego is: ....

....

....

Because: ....

....

....

MORE TO KNOW

....
....
....
....
....
....
....
....
....
....
....
....
....
....
....
....
....
....

....

....

....

....

....

....

....

....

....

....

....

....

....

....

....

....

HOME & AWAY

HOME

A favorite home of mine and why: ....

....

....

....

....

One of my homes looked like this:

Memorable furniture in our home growing up: ....

....

....

....

....

....

When and where I first lived on my own: ....

....

....

....

....

Roommates I have had and what it was like living with them: ....

....

....

....

....

....

....

Where I feel most at home: ....
....
....
....
....
....
....
....

My dream home: ....
....
....
....
....
....
....
....

Places I have lived and what I remember most vividly about them: ....

....

....

....

....

....

....

....

....

If I could live anywhere, it would be: ....

....

....

....

....

....

....

....

....

TRAVEL

Most surprising or unique childhood vacation or outing: ....
....
....
....
....
....
....
....
....

Our greatest family adventure was: ....
....
....
....
....
....
....
....
....

Continents I have visited: ....

....

....

Most far-flung place I have been to: ....

....

....

Places I would still like to visit: ....

....

....

....

....

How travel has impacted my outlook on life: ....

....

....

....

....

....

Memorable trips I have taken: ....
....
....
....
....
....
....
....
....
....
....
....
....
....
....
....

My favorite places in nature: ....

....

....

....

....

....

....

....

The most adventurous thing I have done in the great outdoors: ....

....

....

....

....

....

....

....

National parks or wilderness areas I have visited, and what I remember most: ....

....

....

....

....

The longest journey I have taken: ....
....
....
....
....
....

GETTING AROUND

Our family car growing up: ....
....

My first bicycle: ....
....

My first car: ....
....

How I got to school: ....
....
....

Memorable experiences on a bus, train, plane, or boat: ....
....
....
....
....
....
....
....
....
....

A subway system I am familiar with and the line I most often took: ....
....
....

My favorite mode of transportation: ....
....

MORE TO KNOW

....
....
....
....
....
....
....
....
....
....
....
....
....
....
....
....

CAREER

When and where I had my first job: ....
....
....
....
....

Other jobs I remember: ....
....
....
....
....
....
....
....
....
....
....
....
....
....

My favorite job and why: ....
....
....
....
....
....
....
....
....
....
....

A boss I will never forget and why: ....
....
....
....
....
....
....
....
....
....

My career path and highlights: ....
....
....
....
....
....
....
....
....
....

My definition of success: ....
....
....
....
....
....
....
....
....
....

Mentors in my life: ....

....

....

....

....

....

....

....

....

People and groups I have mentored: ....

....

....

....

....

....

....

....

....

LIVING FULLY

My life in six words: ....
....

What brings me peace or joy about the life I am living: ....
....
....
....
....
....
....
....
....
....
....
....

Hard choices I have made and how they changed my life: ....

....

....

....

....

....

....

....

....

....

....

A time I was at a crossroads and chose the path less traveled: ....

....

....

....

....

....

....

....

....

....

A major life decision I am proud of: ....
....
....
....
....
....
....

A choice I regret: ....
....
....
....
....
....

The biggest risk I have taken and how it turned out: ....
....
....
....
....
....
....
....

The biggest challenge I still face: ....
....
....
....
....

What I am most grateful for: ....
....
....
....
....

My dreams as an adult: ....
....
....
....
....

What I would like people to know about me that they may not: ....
....
....
....
....
....

ACTIVISM & SERVICE

Of the world events that occurred during my lifetime, I most remember: ....

....

....

....

....

....

....

....

....

....

Politicians or political movements that have made a difference in my lifetime: ....

....

....

....

....

....

....

Causes, movements, or campaigns that have meant the most to me: ....

....

....

....

....

....

My military and/or public service and my feelings about serving or not serving: ....

....

....

....

Family members who have been in the military and/or public service: ....

....

....

....

....

....

....

....

MORE TO KNOW

....

....

....

....

....

....

....

....

....

....

....

....

....

....

....

....

....

....

SPIRITUALITY

My spiritual or religious inclination: ....
....

How I came to my beliefs: ....
....
....
....
....

Practices, rituals, or places that make me feel connected to my spirituality: ....
....
....
....
....
....
....
....

My family's religious or spiritual practice: ....
....
....

My favorite quote, teaching, or scripture: ....
....
....
....
....
....
....

How I describe myself and my spiritual life: ....
....
....
....
....
....
....
....
....
....
....

DEATH

What I believe happens when we die: ....
....
....
....
....
....

How I hope to be remembered: ....
....
....
....
....
....
....
....

What I wish I had done more: ....
....
....
....
....

What I wish I had had more of: ....
....
....
....
....

What I would like my funeral or life celebration to look like: ....
....
....
....
....
....
....
....
....
....
....

How I would like to be laid to rest: ....

....

....

....

....

LIFE WISDOM

My personal philosophy on life: ....

....

....

....

....

....

....

....

....

....

....

Things I wish I had known or learned earlier: ....

....

....

....

....

....

....

....

....

My personal philosophy on money: ....

....

....

....

....

....

....

....

....

Things I have learned and would like to pass on: ....
....
....
....
....
....
....
....

What has held meaning in my life: ....
....
....
....
....
....
....
....
....

What I would like my children to know as they make their way through life: ....

....

....

....

....

....

....

....

....

Changes I hope to see in our world in the decades to come: ....

....

....

....

....

....

....

....

....

....

MORE TO KNOW

....
....
....
....
....
....
....
....
....
....
....
....
....
....
....
....
....
....

ABOUT THE AUTHOR

ANNE PHYFE PALMER is an entrepreneur, writer, yogi, and electric-bike commuter who left the swampy heat and Mardi Gras revelry of her hometown of New Orleans and founded 8 Limbs Yoga Centers in Seattle. With this guided journal, Anne Phyfe takes her passion for personal inquiry from the yoga mat to the written word. She lives in Seattle with her family. You can find her at AnnePhyfe.com.

ABOUT THE ARTIST

SARAH TRUMBAUER is a papercut artist and illustrator living in rural eastern Pennsylvania. Her paper cuts are inspired by long walks through gardens, vintage children's books, and art nouveau patterns. Her work has been featured in international magazines, books, and stationery products. When she's not cutting paper, she can be found drinking tea, daydreaming, and reading mystery novels with her cat, Lucy.

Printed in China

SASQUATCH BOOKS with colophon is a registered trademark of
Penguin Random House LLC

27 26 25 24   9 8 7 6 5

Editor: Susan Roxborough | Production editor: Bridget Sweet
Design: Anna Goldstein | Illustrations: Sarah Trumbauer

ISBN: 978-1-63217-208-2

Sasquatch Books
1325 Fourth Avenue, Suite 1025 | Seattle, WA 98101
SasquatchBooks.com